GERMAN
FOR BEGINNERS

Angela Wilkes

Illustrated by John Shackell

Designed by Roger Priddy

Language consultant: Sonja Osthecker

CONTENTS

Handlettering by Jack Potter

About this book

Going abroad is much more fun if you can speak a little of the language. This book shows you that learning another language is a lot easier than you might think. It teaches you the German you will find useful in everyday situations.

You can find out how to . . .

talk about yourself,

and your home,

count and tell the time,

say what you like,

find your way around

and ask for what you want in shops.

How you learn

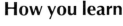

Hallo!

Guten Morgen!

Das ist Peter.

Picture strips like this show you what to say in each situation. Read the speech bubbles and see how much you can understand, then look up any words you do not know. Words and phrases are repeated, to help you remember them. The book starts with easy things to say and gets more difficult towards the end.

New words

All the new words you come across are listed on each double page, so that you can look them up as you go along. If you forget any words you can look them up in the glossary on pages 46-48. *If you see an asterisk by a word, it means that there is a note about it at the bottom of the page.

Grammar

Boxes like this around words show where new grammar is explained. You will find German easier if you learn some of its grammar, or rules, but don't worry if you don't understand it all straightaway. You can find out more about the grammar used in the book on pages 42-43.

Internet links*

At the top of each double page you will find descriptions of useful websites for learning German. For links to these sites, go to **www.usborne-quicklinks.com** and enter the keywords **german for beginners**.

Puzzles

Throughout this book there are puzzles and quizzes to solve (see answers on pages 44-45). You can also find picture puzzles to print out on the Usborne Quicklinks Website at **www.usborne-quicklinks.com**

Practising your German

Write all the new words you learn in a notebook and try to learn a few every day. Keep going over them and you will soon remember them.

Ask a friend to keep testing you on your German. Even better, ask someone to learn German with you so that you can practise on each other.

Try to go to Germany for your holidays, and speak as much German as you can. Don't be afraid of making mistakes. No one will mind.

* For more information on using the Internet, see inside the front cover.

Saying "Hello and Goodbye"

The first things you need to know how to say in German are "Hello" and "How are you?" There are different greetings for different times of day and here you can find out what to say when.

In Germany it is polite to use people's names when you say "Hello" to them. The word for Mr. is **Herr.** The word for Mrs. is **Frau** and Miss is **Fräulein.**

Saying "Hello"

This is what you say when you greet someone you know well.

Guten Tag means "Good day", **Guten Morgen** "Good morning".

This is how you say "Good evening".

Saying "Goodbye"

Tschüs is a friendly way of saying "Goodbye".

These are different ways of saying "See you again".

Saying "Goodnight"

You only say **Gute Nacht** last thing at night.

4   *In Southern Germany people usually say **Grüß Gott** instead.

How are you?

This is how to greet someone and ask how they are.

This person is saying that she is fine, thank you . . .

. . .but this one is saying things aren't too good.

Wie geht's?

This list shows you different ways of saying how you are, from very well to terrible. What do you think each of the people here would say if you asked them how they were?

sehr gut	very well
gut	well
ganz gut	quite well
es geht so	so so
nicht so gut	not very well
furchtbar	terrible

5

What is your name?

Here you can find out how to ask someone their name and tell them yours, and how to introduce your friends. Read the picture strip and see how much you can understand. Then try doing the puzzles on the page opposite.

New Words

ich	I
du	you
er	he
sie	she, they*
wie heißt** du?	what are you called?
ich heiße	I am called
wie heißt er?	what is he called?
er heißt	he is called
sie heißt	she is called
wie heißen sie?	what are they called?
sie heißen	they are called
wer ist das?	who is that?
das ist	this/that is
mein Freund	my friend (male)
meine Freundin	my friend (female)
und	and
ja	yes
nein	no

Saying "you"

In German there are three words for "you" – **du**, **ihr** and **Sie**. You use **du** when talking to someone you know well and **ihr** when you are talking to more than one person. When you talk to adults you don't know well, it is polite to use **Sie**, no matter whether it is one person or more than one. To ask someone's name you would say **Wie heißen Sie?**

Guten Tag. Wie heißt du?

Max, und du?

Ich heiße Monika.

Introducing friends

Das ist mein Freund. Er heißt Peter.

Wer ist das?

Das ist meine Freundin. Sie heißt Sonja.

Wie heißen sie?

Sie heißen Klaus und Daniel.

***Sie** means "she" if the verb ends in 't' and "they" if it ends in 'en' (see page 11).
     **You pronounce ß like 'ss'.

What are they called?
Can you answer these questions in German?

Who is talking to Fritz?
Who is talking to Ingrid?

Who is called Helmut?
Who is talking to him?

Who is called Anita?
Who is going home?

Can you remember?

How would you ask someone their name?
How would you tell them your name?

You have a friend called Anita. How would you introduce her to someone?
How would you tell someone your friend is called Daniel?

Finding out what things are called.

Everything on this picture has its name on it. They all begin with a capital letter because in German all nouns (names of things) do. Learn as many of them as you can, then try the test on the opposite page.

der Schornstein

das Dach

die Sonne

der Vogel

das Nest

Guten Tag!

der Baum

das Fenster

die Blumen

die Katze

das Haus

Das ist mein Haus.

die Tür

die Garage

der Zaun

der Hund

das Auto

Der, die and das words

In German, nouns are either masculine, feminine or neuter. The word for "the" is **der** before masculine nouns, **die** before feminine nouns and **das** before neuter ones. It is best to learn which word to use with each noun. The German for "a" or "an" is **ein** before **der** and **das** words and **eine** before **die** words.

der Schornstein	chimney	**die**	**Katze**	cat	**das**	**Dach**	roof
(ein) Vogel	bird	**(eine)**	**Tür**	door	**(ein)**	**Haus**	house
Baum	tree		**Garage**	garage		**Nest**	nest
Hund	dog		**Sonne**	sun		**Fenster**	window
Zaun	fence		**Blume**	flower		**Auto**	car

Asking what things are called

Don't worry if you don't know the word for something in German. You can always ask what it is. Look at the list of useful phrases below, then read the picture strip to see how to use them.

was ist das?	what is that?
das ist . . .	that is . . .
wie heißt das?	what is that called?
das heißt . . .	that is called . . .
auf deutsch	in German
auf englisch	in English

Was ist das?

Das ist eine Blume.

Ist das auch eine Blume?

Nein, das ist ein Baum!

Wie heißt das auf deutsch?

Das heißt eine Tür.

Und wie heißt das?

Das heißt ein Hund.

Wie heißt das auf englisch?

A dog!

Can you remember?

Cover up the opposite page and see if you can name these things in German. Don't forget to say whether they are **der, die** or **das** words.

9

Where do you come from?

Here you can find out how to ask people where they come from, where they live, and tell them where you live. You can also find out how to ask if they speak German.

New words

woher kommst du?	where do you come from?
ich komme aus	I come from
wo wohnst du?	where do you live?
ich wohne in . . .	I live in
sprichst du . . .?	do you speak . . .?
ich spreche . . .	I speak . . .
ein bisschen	a little
Deutsch	German
Englisch	English
Französisch	French

Countries

Afrika	Africa
Deutschland	Germany
England	England
Frankreich	France
Indien	India
Schottland	Scotland
Österreich	Austria
Spanien	Spain
Ungarn	Hungary

Where do you come from?

Do you speak German?

Who comes from where?

These are the contestants for an international dancing competition. They all come from different countries. The compère only speaks English and does not understand where anyone comes from. Can you tell him what he wants to know? His questions are below the picture.

Angus kommt aus Schottland.

Das sind Marie und Pierre. Sie kommen aus Frankreich.

Hari und Indira kommen aus Indien.

Yuri kommt aus Ungarn. Er wohnt in Budapest.

Franz kommt aus Österreich.

Das ist Lolita. Sie kommt aus Spanien.

Where do they all come from?

Where does Franz come from?
What are the Indian contestants called?
Are there any French contestants?
Is Lolita Italian?

Where do Hari and Indira come from?
Is there a Scottish contestant?
Where does Pierre come from?
Who lives in Budapest?

Verbs

German verbs (action words) change their endings according to who is doing the action. Most of them, like kommen (to come) and wohnen (to live), follow a regular pattern and have the same endings. You can see what they are on the right*.

kommen	to come
ich komme	I come
du kommst	you come
er kommt	he comes
sie kommt	she comes
wir kommen	we come
sie kommen	they come

Can you remember?

How would you ask someone where they come from?

Can you say where you come from?
How do you say that you speak German?
How would you ask someone if they can?

*You can see how **sprechen** changes on pages 42-43.

More about you

Here you can find out how to count up to 20, say how old you are and say how many brothers and sisters you have.

New words

wie alt . . .	how old . . .
bist du?	are you?
ich bin . . .	I am . . .
. . .Jahre alt	. . .years old
hast du . . .?	have you . . .?
ich habe	I have
die Geschwister	brothers and sisters
der Bruder	brother
die Schwester	sister
fast	almost
keine	not any
wir	we
ihr	you (plural)
aber	but

Plural words

Most German nouns change in the plural (when there is more than one person or thing). You add a letter or letters to some words, e.g. **Schwestern** (sisters) and an umlaut (¨) to some others, e.g. **Brüder** (brothers).

The word for "the" is always **die** before plural nouns. The plurals of all the words in the book are listed in the glossary on page 46.

Numbers

1	eins	11	elf
2	zwei	12	zwölf
3	drei	13	dreizehn
4	vier	14	vierzehn
5	fünf	15	fünfzehn
6	sechs	16	sechzehn
7	sieben	17	siebzehn
8	acht	18	achtzehn
9	neun	19	neunzehn
10	zehn	20	zwanzig

How old are you?

Have you any brothers and sisters?

12

How old are they?

Read what these children are saying, then see if you can say how old they all are.

Boris ist zwölf.

Wir sind fünfzehn.

Kirsten ist elf Jahre alt.

Michael ist fast vierzehn.

Ich bin fünf. Er ist neun.

Michael   Petra und Sabine   Boris   Kirsten   Hugo   Barbara

How many brothers and sisters?

Below you can read how many brothers and sisters the children have. Can you work out who has which brothers and sisters?

Petra und Sabine haben einen Bruder und zwei Schwestern.

Kirsten hat drei Schwestern und zwei Brüder.

Michael hat fünf Schwestern aber keine Brüder.

Hugo hat einen Bruder aber keine Schwester.

Boris hat keine Geschwister aber er hat einen Hund.

A

B

D

C

E

Useful verbs

sein	to be
ich bin	I am
du bist	you are
er/sie/es ist	he/she/it is
wir sind	we are
ihr seid	you are
Sie sind	you are
sie sind	they are

haben	to have
ich habe	I have
du hast	you have
er/sie/es hat	he/she/it has
wir haben	we have
ihr habt	you have
Sie haben	you have
sie haben	they have

Talking about your family

On these two pages you will learn lots of words which will help you to talk about your family. You will also find out how to say "my" and "your" and describe people.

Das ist meine Familie.

mein Groβvater*

mein Vater

meine Schwester

mein Onkel

meine Katze

mein Hund

meine Groβmutter

meine Mutter

mein Bruder

meine Tante

Who's who?

Ist das dein Bruder?

Ja, das ist mein Bruder.

Und ist das deine Schwester?

Ja, sie heiβt Tina.

Sind das deine Eltern?

Nein! Das sind meine Groβeltern!

New words

German	English	German	English	German	English
die Familie	family	**die Tante**	aunt	**dick**	fat
der Groβvater*	grandfather	**die Groβeltern**	grandparents	**schlank**	thin
die Groβmutter	grandmother	**die Eltern**	parents	**alt**	old
der Vater	father	**groβ**	tall	**jung**	young
die Mutter	mother	**aber**	but	**blond**	blonde
der Onkel	uncle	**klein**	small	**dunkelhaarig**	dark-haired
		sehr nett	very nice	**freundlich**	friendly

How to say "my" and "your"

For **der** and **das** words the word for "my" is **mein**. For "your" it is **dein**. Before **die** words it is **meine** or **deine**.

	my	your
der words	**mein**	**dein**
die words	**meine**	**deine**
das words	**mein**	**dein**
plurals	**meine**	**deine**

*To say "Grandfather" to someone, you just say "**Groβvater**".

Describing your family

Mein Vater ist groß aber meine Mutter ist klein.

Meine Eltern sind sehr nett.

Mein Onkel ist dick aber meine Tante ist schlank.

Meine Großeltern sind alt. Ich bin jung.

Meine Schwester ist blond. Mein Bruder ist dunkelhaarig.

Mein Hund ist freundlich!

Can you describe them?

Can you describe these people in German, using the new words you have learnt? Start each description **Er ist . . .** or **Sie ist** . . . (He is or she is). Use as many words as you can to describe each person, e.g. **Er ist groß, jung und blond.** (He is tall, young and fair).

Can you describe yourself and your family?

Your home

Here you can find out how to say what sort of home you live in and whether it is in a town or the country. You can also learn what all the rooms in a house are called.

New words

oder	or
das Haus	house
die Wohnung	flat
das Schloss	castle
in der Stadt	in the town
auf dem Land	in the country
am Meer	by the sea
Vati	Dad
Mutti	Mum
Opa	Grandad
Oma	Granny
das Gespenst	ghost
wo seid ihr alle?	where are you all?
das Zimmer	room
das Badezimmer	bathroom
das Esszimmer	dining room
das Schlafzimmer	bedroom
das Wohnzimmer	living room
die Küche	kitchen
der Flur	hall
oben	upstairs
hier	here

Where do you live?

Wohnst du in einem Haus oder in einer Wohnung?

Ich wohne in einem Haus.

Ich wohne in einer Wohnung.

Ich wohne in einem Schloss.

Town or country?

Ich wohne in der Stadt.

Ich wohne auf dem Land

Ich wohne am Meer.

Where is everyone?

Dad comes home and wants to know where everyone is. Look at the pictures and see if you can tell him where all the family are, e.g. **Oma** **ist im Wohnzimmer**. Then see if you can answer the questions below the little pictures.

Wer ist im Esszimmer?
Wer ist in der Küche?
Wer ist im Badezimmer?
Wer ist im Schlafzimmer?

Wo ist Oma?
Wo ist das Gespenst?
Wo ist der Hund?
Wo ist Peter?

How would you tell someone you were upstairs?
How would you tell them you were in the kitchen?

What does "dem" mean?*

In German, words like 'in' and 'on', which tell you where things are, change the word that comes after them.

der becomes **dem**
die becomes **der**
das becomes **dem**
(**in dem** is shortened to **im**)

Ein and eine change like this:
ein becomes einem
eine becomes einer

*You can read more about this on pages 42-43.

Looking for things

Here you can find out how to ask someone what they are looking for and tell them where things are. You can also learn lots of words for things around the house.

New words

da	there
suchen	to look for
etwas	something
der Hamster	hamster
finden	to find
ihn	him/it
auf	on
unter	under
hinter	behind
vor	in front of
zwischen	between
neben	next to
der Schrank	cupboard
der Sessel	armchair
der Vorhang	curtain
die Topfblume	pot plant
das Bücherregal	bookshelf
der Tisch	table
der Teppich	carpet
das Sofa	sofa
der Fernseher	television
das Telefon	telephone
die Vase	vase

Er, sie or es?

The word you use for "it" depends on whether the word it replaces is a **der**, **die** or **das** word. You use **er** for **der** words, **sie** for **die** words and **es** for **das** words.

Wo ist **der** Hamster?
Er ist da.

Wo ist **die** Katze?
Sie ist da.

Wo ist **das** Kätzchen?
Es ist da.

The missing hamster

Suchst du etwas?

Ich suche meinen* Hamster. Ich finde ihn nicht!

Er ist nicht auf dem Schrank.

Er ist nicht unter dem Sofa

Ist er hinter dem Vorhang?

Nein.

Er ist da! Zwischen den Blumen!

*You can find out why **mein** sometimes becomes **meinen** on page 32.

In, on or under?

Der, die, das and **ein** change if they come after any of these words, as you can see on the opposite page. You can check how they change on page 17.

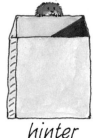

in   *hinter*   *vor*   *neben*   *unter*   *auf*

Where are they hiding?

Herr Boll has six pets but he cannot find them. Can you tell him where they are in German, using the words above? Remember to use **dem** and **der** after them.

der Hamster

das Kätzchen

das Hündchen

der Wellensittich

die Schlange

die Schildkröte

das Bücherregal

der Schrank

der Fernseher

der Teppich

die Vase

das Telefon

der Tisch

der Sessel

das Sofa

What do you like eating?

Here you can find out how to say what you like and don't like. You will also learn lots of food words.

New words

magst du . . .?	do you like . . .?
ich mag . . .	I like . . .
ich mag . . . nicht	I don't like
gar nicht	not at all
sehr gern	very much
lieber	better
am liebsten	best
der Salat	salad
der Fisch	fish
die Pommes frites	chips
der Kuchen	cake
die Würstchen	sausages
das Steak	steak
die Spaghetti	spaghetti
essen	to eat
die Pizza	pizza
der Hamburger	hamburger
ich auch	me too

Saying "I do not like"

In German the word for "not" is **nicht** and you say it after the thing you don't like, e.g. **Ich mag Fisch nicht.**

What do you like?

Magst du Salat?

Nein, ich mag Salat nicht.

Magst du Fisch?

Nein, gar nicht.

Also, was magst du?

Ich mag Pommes Frites.

Und ich mag Kuchen sehr gern

What do you like best?

Was magst du am liebsten?

Ich mag Würstchen sehr gern

. . . Aber ich mag Steak lieber

Und am liebsten mag ich Spaghetti!

What are they eating?

Was isst du?

Ich esse eine Pizza.

Sie isst Pommes frites!

Er isst Brot un Käse.

Wir essen Hamburger.

Ihr esst Reis.

Sie essen Bananen.

Who likes what?

Look at what everyone is saying, then try the questions below the picture. You can find out which of the food words are **der, die** or **das** words in the glossary at the back of the book.

Ich auch, aber ich mag Schinken nicht.

Johann

Ich mag Bananen!

Stefan

Ich mag Trauben lieber.

Opa

Ich mag Käse.

Boris

Ich mag Obsttorte am liebsten!

Heidi

Schinken Butter Quiche

Brot Salat Tomaten Käse

Bananen Trauben Obsttorte Orangensaft

Who likes cheese?
Who doesn't like ham?
What is the gorilla eating?
Who prefers grapes to bananas?
What does Heidi like best?

Can you say in German which things you like and which you don't like?
Cover up the picture and see if you can remember the words for ham, cheese, bread, butter and fruit tart.

21

Table talk

Here you can learn all sorts of useful things to say if you are having a meal with German friends.

New words

zu Tisch bitte	come to the table please
ich habe Hunger	I'm hungry
ich auch	me too
bedien dich	help yourself
bedient euch	help yourselves
guten Appetit	enjoy your meal
danke gleichfalls	the same to you
kannst du mir . . . reichen	can you pass me . . .
das Wasser	water
das Brot	bread
das Glas	glass
möchten Sie /möchtest du noch . . . ?	would you like some more . . . ?
das Fleisch	meat
ja bitte	yes please
nein danke	no, thank you
das reicht	I've had enough
schmeckt's?	is it good?
es schmeckt sehr gut	it's delicious

Dinner is ready

Zu Tisch bitte!

Ich habe Hunger.

Ich auch!

Bedien dich bitte.

Danke.

Guten Appetit!

Danke gleichfalls!

Please will you pass me . . .

Kannst du mir bitte das Wasser reichen?

Kannst du mir bitte das Brot reichen?

Kannst du mir ein Glas reichen?

Would you like some more?

Who is saying what?

These little pictures show you different mealtime situations. Cover up the rest of the page and see if you know what everyone would say in German.

Stefan is saying he is hungry.

The chef wants you to enjoy your meal.

Heidi wants her friend to help himself.

Peter wants someone to pass him a glass.

Mum is offering Stefan more chips.

He says "yes please" and that he likes chips.

Then he says "No thanks", he's had enough.

Boris is saying the food is delicious.

Den and einen

When the object of a verb (the thing or person the action affects) is a **der** word, the word for "the" or "a" changes:

der becomes **den** and **ein** becomes **einen**:
Ich esse den Kuchen (I am eating the cake)
Ich habe einen Bruder (I have a brother).*

*You can find out more about this on page 42.

Your hobbies

All these people are talking about their hobbies and the things they like doing.

New words

machen	to do
malen	to paint
kochen	to cook
basteln	to make things
tanzen	to dance
lesen	to read
fernsehen*	to watch TV
stricken	to knit
gehen	to go
schwimmen	to swim
spielen	to play
das Hobby	hobby
der Sport	sport
der Fußball	football
das Tennis	tennis
die Musik	music
hören	to listen to
das Instrument	instrument
die Geige	violin
das Klavier	piano
abends	in the evenings

Verbs

Some verbs do not follow the regular pattern and it is best to learn them. Here is how **lesen** changes:

lesen	to read
ich lese	I read
du liest	you read
er/sie liest	he/she reads
wir lesen	we read
ihr lest	you read (pl)
Sie lesen	you read
sie lesen	they read

gern

To say someone likes (or doesn't like) doing something you put **gern** (or **nicht gern**) after the verb.

Was machst du gern?

Ich male gern...

Aber ich koche nicht gern.

Was sind deine Hobbys?

Ich bastele gern...

Und ich tanze gern.

What do you do in the evenings?

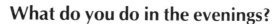

Was machst du abends?

Ich lese Bücher...

Oder ich sehe fern und ich stricke.

*To say "I watch television" you say **ich sehe fern**.

The sporty type

Hast du Hobbys?

Ich mag Sport!

Ich gehe schwimmen.

Ich spiele Fußball...

und ich spiele Tennis.

Music lovers

Habt ihr Hobbys?

Ja, wir hören gern Musik.

Spielt ihr Instrumente?

Und ich spiele Klavier.

Ja, ich spiele Geige.

What are they doing?

A

B

C

D

E

Cover up the rest of the page and see if you can say what all these people are doing in German e.g. **Er spielt Fußball.** Can you say what your hobbies are?

Telling the time

Here you can find out how to tell the time using the 12 hour clock, which is what the Germans use for everyday speech. You can look up any numbers you don't know on page 40.

In German, to say "half past" you say "half to" the next hour, e.g. for "half past nine" you say **halb zehn**, meaning half to ten.

New words

wie spät ist es?	what is the time?
wie viel Uhr ist es?	what is the time?
es ist ein Uhr	it is one o'clock
nach/vor	past/to
Viertel nach	quarter past
Viertel vor	quarter to
halb	half past
Mittag	midday
Mitternacht	midnight
morgens	in the morning
abends	in the evening
um	at
aufstehen	to get up
sein	his
das Frühstück	breakfast
das Mittagessen	lunch
das Abendessen	supper/tea
zur Schule	to school
zu Bett	to bed

Word order

In German sentences the verb always comes second. Usually the person or thing doing the action comes first, e.g. **Hugo geht zu Bett** (Hugo goes to bed), but when you talk about time, the time goes first, so you swap the verb and its subject round, e.g. **Um acht Uhr geht Hugo zu Bett**.

What is the time?

These are the two ways you can ask what the time is.

The time is . . .

Es ist fünf nach neun.

Es ist Viertel nach neun.

Es ist halb zehn.

Es ist Viertel vor zehn.

Es ist fünf vor zehn.

Es ist Mittag/ Mitternacht.

What time of day is it?*

Es ist sechs Uhr morgens.

Es ist sechs Uhr abends.

*For "in the afternoon" you say **nachmittags**.

Hugo's day

Read what Hugo does, then see if you can

match each clock with the right picture. You will find the answers on page 45.

a   b   c   d   e   f   g   h

1

Hugo steht um halb acht auf.*

2

Um acht Uhr ißt er sein Frühstück.

3

Um Viertel vor neun geht er zur Schule.

4

Um halb eins ißt er sein Mittagessen.

5

Um zehn nach zwei spielt er Fußball.

6

Um Viertel nach fünf sieht er fern.

7

Um sechs Uhr ißt er sein Abendessen.

8

Um halb neun geht er zu Bett.

What time is it?

Can you say in German what times these watches and clocks show?

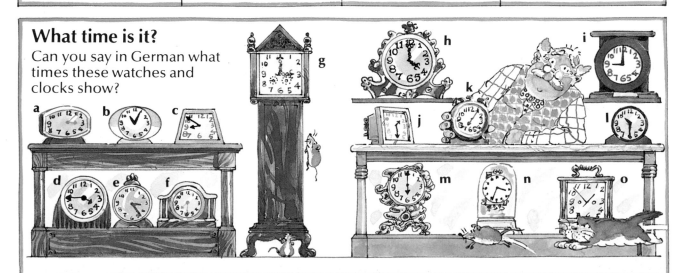

*__Aufstehen__ splits into two parts when you use it. You use __stehen__ like an ordinary verb, but __auf__ goes to the end of the sentence.

Arranging things

Here you can find out how to arrange things with your German friends.

New words

wann?	when?
am Dienstag	on Tuesday
am Morgen /Nachmittag	in the morning /afternoon
am Abend	in the evening
prima	that's great
bis dann	until then
heute	today
heute Abend	this evening
bis morgen*	until tomorrow
das geht	that's fine
das geht nicht	that's no good
schade!	it's a pity!
ins Kino gehen	to go to the cinema
in die Disko gehen	to go to the disco
auf eine Party gehen	to go to a party

Days of the week

Sonntag	Sunday
Montag	Monday
Dienstag	Tuesday
Mittwoch	Wednesday
Donnerstag	Thursday
Freitag	Friday
Samstag	Saturday

Tennis

Swimming

Going to the cinema

28   *Do not confuse **morgen** (tomorrow) with **der Morgen** (morning).

Going to a party

Kommst du auf meine Party?

Wann?

Am Samstag-abend.

Schade, das geht nicht.

Am Samstag gehe ich in die Disko.

Your diary for the week

Here is your diary, showing you what you are doing for a week. Read what it says, then see if you can answer the questions at the bottom of the page.

Montag
4 Uhr. Tennis

Dienstag
2 Uhr. Klavier
5.30 Schwimmen

Mittwoch
3 Uhr. Tennis
7.45 Kino

Donnerstag

Freitag
8 Uhr. Disko mit Boris

Samstag
2 Uhr. Fußball
7 Uhr. Party.

Sonntag
Tennis—Nachmittag

What are you doing on Friday evening?
When are you playing tennis?
When are you going to the cinema?
Have you a piano lesson on Tuesday?
Are you free on Sunday morning?
What time is the party on Saturday?

Boris asks you to go swimming with him on Saturday afternoon. What do you say to him?

Anja asks you to a concert on Thursday evening. What do you say to her?

Asking where places are

Here and on the next two pages you can find out how to ask your way around in Germany.

Always be polite when you are asking people the way and say **Sie** to them rather than **du**.

New words

Entschuldigung	excuse me
bitte schön	not at all
hier	here
die Post	post office
am Marktplatz	in the market place
auf der rechten Seite	on the right
auf der linken Seite	on the left
das Hotel	hotel
dann	then
gibt es . . .?	is . . . there?
in der Nähe	nearby
die Straße	road, street
gleich	immediately
ist es weit?	is it far?
etwa	about
die Minute	minute
zu Fuß	on foot
der Supermarkt	supermarket
da drüben	over there
gegenüber	opposite
neben	next to
die Bank	bank
die Apotheke	chemist's

Being polite

> *Entschuldigung...*

This is how to say "Excuse me" before you ask someone something.

> *Danke schön*

> *Bitte schön*

When you thank someone they may answer **bitte, bitte schön** or **bitte sehr.**

Where is . . .?

> *Entschuldigung, wo ist hier die Post?*

> *Am Marktplatz, auf der rechten Seite.*

> *Wo ist das Hotel Adler bitte?*

> *Gehen Sie hier rechts und dann geradeaus.*

Directions

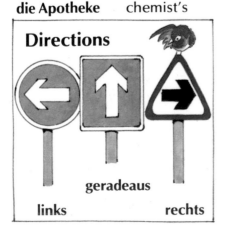

geradeaus

links   rechts

Internet links For links to websites where you can discover Germany with a clickable map and follow an online lesson about asking directions, **go to www.usborne-quicklinks.com**

Is there a . . . nearby?

Is it far?

Other useful places to ask for

der Bahnhof	eine Tankstelle	die Toiletten	ein Briefkasten
station	petrol station	toilets	letter box
eine Telefonzelle	der Campingplatz	das Krankenhaus	der Flughafen
telephone box	campsite	hospital	airport

Finding your way around

Here you can find out how to ask your way around and follow directions. When you have read everything, try the map puzzle on the opposite page.

Entschuldigung Wie komme ich zum Bahnhof, bitte?

Nehmen Sie die erste Straße rechts und die zweite Straße links.

Der Bahnhof ist auf der rechten Seite.

Wie komme ich bitte zur Jugendherberge?

Gehen Sie diese Straße entlang bis zum Bahnhof...

dann nehmen Sie die dritte Straße rechts.

Wie komme ich bitte zum Verkehrsamt?

Mit dem Auto? Fahren* Sie hier um die Ecke...

dann nehmen Sie die nächste Straße links.

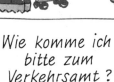

*When someone is in a car, you use the word **fahren** for "to go".

New words

wie komme ich zum/zur ...?	how do I get to ...?	**bis zum/zur**	as far as
nehmen Sie ...	take ...	**mit dem Auto**	by car
fahren Sie ...	drive ...	**um die Ecke**	round the corner
die Jugendherberge	youth hostel	**die erste Straße**	the first street
das Verkehrsamt	tourist office	**die zweite Straße**	the second street
die Straße entlang	along the road	**die dritte Straße**	the third street
		die nächste Straße	the next street

Zum and zur

When you ask the way in German you say **wie komme ich zum ...?** or **wie komme ich zur ...?***

You use **zum** with **der** and **das** words:
wie komme ich zum Bahnhof?
wie komme ich zum Café

and **zur** with **die** words:
wie komme ich zur Post?
wie komme ich zur Kirche?

Finding your way around Dimbstal.

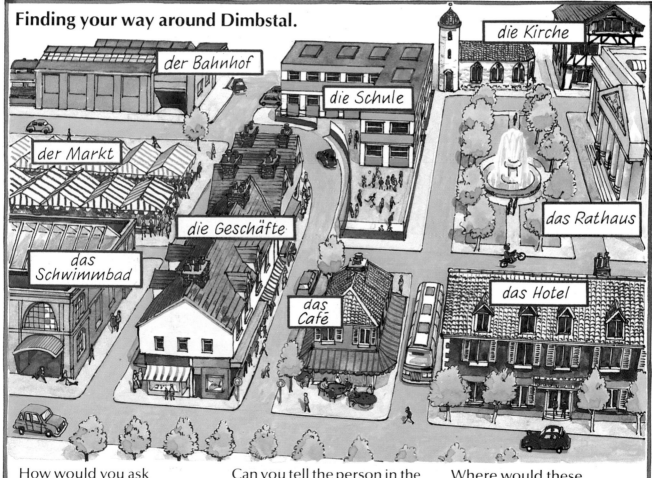

How would you ask someone the way to the market place?
How would you ask them if there is a cafe nearby?

Can you tell the person in the yellow car how to get to the church?
Can you direct someone from the hotel to the market?

Where would these directions take the yellow car? **Nehmen Sie die zweite Straße links, und sie sind auf der linken Seite.**

---

*When you ask your way to a town, you use **nach**, e.g. **Wie komme ich nach London?**

Going shopping

Here and on the next two pages you can find out how to say what you want when you go shopping.

Spending money

There are 100 **Cent** in a **Euro**. On price labels, the symbol € is used before the price. For example, **zwei Euro** is written as €2, and **zwei Euro zwanzig** as €2.20. To understand prices you must know the numbers in German. They are listed on page 40.

Frau Voss goes shopping

Frau Voss geht einkaufen.

Sie kauft Brötchen in der Bäckerei.

New words

einkaufen gehen	to go shopping
kaufen	to buy
die Bäckerei	baker's
das Lebens– mittelgeschäft	grocer's
die Metzgerei	butcher's
die Milch	milk
die Eier	eggs
das Obst	fruit
die Gemüse	vegetables
das Fleisch	meat
das Brötchen	bread roll
die Äpfel	apples
die Tomaten	tomatoes
bitte schön?	can I help you?
was darf es sein?	can I help you?
ich möchte	I would like
ich hätte gern	I would like
gerne	with pleasure
sonst noch etwas?	anything else?
außerdem noch etwas?	anything else?
was macht das?	what does that come to?
...zusammen	...altogether
ein Kilo	a kilo
ein Pfund	half a kilo

In der Bäckerei

Guten Tag.

Guten Tag. Bitte schön?

Ich möchte vier Brötchen.

Gerne. Sonst noch etwas?

Nein, danke. Was macht das?

Drei Euro

Bitte schön.

Sie kauft Milch und Eier im Lebensmittelgeschäft.

Sie kauft Obst und Gemüse auf dem Markt.

Sie kauft Fleisch in der Metzgerei.

Im Lebensmittelgeschäft

Bitte schön?

Ich hätte gern sechs Eier bitte.

Außerdem noch etwas?

Ja, ein Liter Milch, bitte.

Was macht das zusammen?

Zwei Euro zwanzig, bitte.

Auf dem Markt.

Guten Tag. Was darf es sein?

Ich möchte ein Kilo Äpfel, bitte.

Sonst noch etwas?

Ja, ein Pfund Tomaten.

Also, das macht zusammen vier Euro.

€4

More shopping and going to a café

Here you can find out how to ask how much things cost and how to order things in a café.

New words

kosten	to cost
was kostet /kosten . . .?	..how much is . . /are . . .?
die Postkarte	postcard
. . .das Kilo	. . .a kilo
. . .das Stück	. . .each
die Rose	rose
der Kaffee	coffee
zahlen bitte!	please may I pay!
die Traube	grape
die Orange	orange
die Banane	banana
die Ananas	pineapple
die Zitrone	lemon
der Pfirsich	peach
die Limonade	lemonade
die Cola	coca cola
der Tee	tea
mit Milch	with milk
mit Zitrone	with lemon
heiße Schokolade	hot chocolate
ein Glas . . .	a glass of
die Milch	milk
das Eis	ice cream

Asking how much things cost

Was kostet eine Postkarte bitte ?

Sechzig Cent.

Was kosten die Trauben bitte ?

Zwei Euro dreißig das Kilo.

€2.30

Was kosten die Rosen bitte ?

Drei Euro zehn das Stück.

€3.10

Also, sieben Stück, bitte.

Going to a café

Bitte schön?

Ich möchte einen Kaffee bitte.

Bitte schön.

Danke.

Zahlen bitte !

Das macht drei Euro.

*Ein Stück means one of something, so if you want seven of something, you just say sieben Stück.

Internet links *For links to websites where you can watch a video on shopping at a market and follow a conversation at a snack bar,* **go to** *www.usborne-quicklinks.com*

Buying fruit

Everything on the fruit stall is marked with its name and price.

Look at the picture, then see if you can answer the questions below it.

ÄPFEL
Kilo
€1.80

Bitte schön.

BANANEN
Kilo
€1.70

TRAUBEN
Kilo
€2.30

ORANGEN
Kilo
€1.90

ANANAS
Stück
€2

PFIRSICHE
Kilo
€2.10

ZITRONEN
Stück
€0.40

How do you tell the stallholder you would like four lemons, a kilo of bananas and a pineapple? Can you see how much these things cost?

Was kostet zwei Euro das Stück?
Was kostet zwei Euro zehn das Kilo?
Was kostet zwei Euro dreizig das Kilo?
Was kostet vierzig Cent das Stück?

Things to order

Here are some things you might want to order in a café.

Ich möchte..

| *eine Limonade* | *eine Cola* | *einen Tee mit Milch* | *einen Tee mit Zitrone* |
| *einen Orangensaft* | *eine heiße Schokolade* | *ein Glas Milch* | *ein Eis* |

37

The months and seasons

Here you can learn what the seasons and months are called and find out how to say what date it is.

New words

der Monat	month
das Jahr	year
welches Datum haben wir?	what is the date?
heute	today
der Geburtstag	birthday

The seasons

der Frühling	spring
der Sommer	summer
der Herbst	autumn
der Winter	winter

The months

Januar	January
Februar	February
März	March
April	April
Mai	May
Juni	June
Juli	July
August	August
September	September
Oktober	October
November	November
Dezember	December

The seasons

der Frühling

März, April, Mai ...

der Sommer

Juni, Juli, August...

der Herbst

September, Oktober, November...

der Winter

Dezember, Januar, Februar...

First, second, third . . .

To say 'first', 'second', etc. you add **te** to numbers up to 19, e.g.
der/die/das zweite
der/die/das neunzehnte
The only exceptions are **erste** (first), **dritte** (third), **siebte** (seventh) and **achte** (eighth).

You add **ste** to all numbers from 20 onwards, e.g. **der/die/das zwanzigste**

Januar ist der erste Monat im* Jahr.

Februar ist der zweite Monat im Jahr.

Dezember ist der zwölfte Monat im Jahr.

Can you say where the rest of the months come in the year?

*Remember: **im** is short for **in dem** (in the).

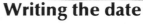

What is the date?

Heute haben wir den dritten Mai

Welches Datum haben wir heute?

Den* ersten Januar.

Writing the date

Berlin, den 3. Mai

When you write a date down, for example at the top of a letter, you just put a dot after the number.

When is your birthday?

Wann hast du Geburtstag?

Am zehnten November.

Mein Geburtstag ist am zwölften Februar.

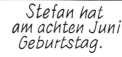

Stefan hat am achten Juni Geburtstag.

Am means 'on the'. As with the dates above, you add 'n' to the number.

When are their birthdays?

The date of each person's birthday is written below them. Can you say in German when their birthdays are, e.g. **Karin hat am zweiten April Geburtstag.**

Karin	Hans	Astrid	Monika	Karl	Klaus

2. April.	21. Juli.	18. Oktober.	31. August.	3. März.	7. September

*You say **den** here and add **'n'** to the number.

Colours and numbers

Colours are describing words, like 'big' and 'small', and you use them in the same way,

Internet links For links to websites with lots of online exercises and listening games on colours and numbers, go to www.usborne-quicklinks.com

e.g. **die Katze ist schwarz** (the cat is black).

The colours

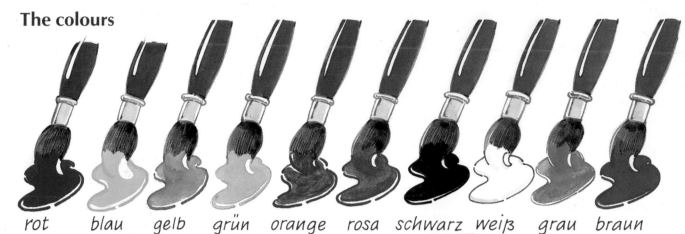

rot   blau   gelb   grün   orange   rosa   schwarz   weiß   grau   braun

What colour is it?

Cover the picture above and see if you can say what colour everything is in the painting. You should know all the words you need.*

Numbers

You will see that from 13 onwards you put the units before the tens, e.g. **zweiundzwanzig** (two and twenty). You count from 30 to 39 etc. in the same way as from 20 to 29.

1 eins	11 elf	21 einundzwanzig	31 einunddreißig
2 zwei	12 zwölf	22 zweiundzwanzig	40 vierzig
3 drei	13 dreizehn	23 dreiundzwanzig	50 fünfzig
4 vier	14 vierzehn	24 vierundzwanzig	60 sechzig
5 fünf	15 fünfzehn	25 fünfundzwanzig	70 siebzig
6 sechs	16 sechzehn	26 sechsundzwanzig	80 achtzig
7 sieben	17 siebzehn	27 siebenundzwanzig	90 neunzig
8 acht	18 achtzehn	28 achtundzwanzig	100 hundert
9 neun	19 neunzehn	29 neunundzwanzig	101 hunderteins
10 zehn	20 zwanzig	30 dreißig	200 zweihundert

*The sky is **der Himmel**.

Pronunciation Guide

The best way to learn to speak German is to listen carefully to German people and copy what they say, but here are some general points to help you.

Below is a list of the main letters which sound different in German from in English, with a guide on how to say each one. For each German word we have shown an English word, or part of a word, which sounds like it. Read it out aloud in a normal way to find out how to pronounce the German sound, then practise saying the examples shown beneath.

a
When it is short it is like the "a" in "cat":
d<u>a</u>nke, T<u>a</u>sse, St<u>a</u>dt, B<u>a</u>ll

When it is long it is like the "ar" sound in "cart":
V<u>a</u>ter, f<u>a</u>hren, B<u>a</u>hnhof

ä
Like the "a" in "care":
sp<u>ä</u>t, L<u>ä</u>rm, K<u>ä</u>se, B<u>ä</u>r

au
Like the "ow" sound in "cow":
Fr<u>au</u>, <u>au</u>f, b<u>au</u>en

äu, eu
Like the "oy" sound in "toy":
Fr<u>äu</u>lein, Fr<u>eu</u>nd, h<u>eu</u>te

ö
Like the "u" sound in "fur":
<u>ö</u>ffnen, h<u>ö</u>ren, m<u>ö</u>chte, zw<u>ö</u>lf

ü
Round your lips as if to say "oo", then try to say "ee":
<u>ü</u>ber, f<u>ü</u>r, k<u>ü</u>ssen, T<u>ü</u>r

ei
Like the "i" in "fine":
n<u>ei</u>n, G<u>ei</u>ge, m<u>ei</u>sten, R<u>ei</u>he

ie
Like the "ee" sound in "feel":
T<u>ie</u>r, s<u>ie</u>ben, fl<u>ie</u>gen, Sp<u>ie</u>l

ch
A soft sound like the "ch" in the Scottish word "loch":
i<u>ch</u>, Bu<u>ch</u>, ma<u>ch</u>en, a<u>ch</u>t

d
Like the English "d" except at the end of a word, where it is "t":
<u>d</u>ort, <u>D</u>ing, un<u>d</u>, Mon<u>d</u>, Gel<u>d</u>

g
Like the "g" in "garden" except after "i", where it is like the German "ch" above:
<u>G</u>eld, <u>G</u>arten, We<u>g</u>, schmutzi<u>g</u>

j
Like the "y" in "yellow":
<u>j</u>a, <u>J</u>unge, <u>J</u>acke

sch
Like the "sh" sound in "shirt":
<u>sch</u>ön, <u>Sch</u>okolade, <u>sch</u>nell

sp, st
These sound like "shp" and "sht" when they are at the beginning of a word:
<u>Sp</u>iegel, <u>sp</u>rechen, <u>St</u>uhl, <u>St</u>adt

s
Like "z" when it comes before a vowel:
<u>s</u>ehen, <u>s</u>itzen, <u>S</u>and, lang<u>s</u>am

Before other letters, or at the end of a word, it is like the "s" in "soap":
da<u>s</u>, Gla<u>s</u>, etwa<u>s</u>, Ne<u>s</u>t

ß
This is like "ss":
Fu<u>ß</u>ball, Stra<u>ß</u>e

v
Like the "f" in "friend":
<u>v</u>on, <u>v</u>iel, <u>V</u>ater

w
Like the "v" in "van":
<u>W</u>asser, <u>w</u>arm, <u>w</u>er, <u>W</u>ort

z
Like the "ts" in "hits":
<u>z</u>u, Her<u>z</u>, <u>z</u>usammen, <u>Z</u>unge

German grammar

Internet links *For links to websites where you can conjugate German verbs online and find an online guide to German grammar,* **go to** *www.usborne-quicklinks.com*

Grammar is like a set of rules about how you put words together and it is different for every language. You will find German easier if you learn some of its grammar, but don't worry if you don't understand it all straightaway. Just read a little about it at a time. This is a summary of the grammar used in this book.

Nouns

A noun is the name of something, such as a dog, a flower or a horse. In German every noun begins with a capital letter and has a gender. This means that it is either masculine (m), feminine (f) or neuter (n). The word you use for "the" shows which gender the noun is, so it is a good idea to learn which word to use with each noun.

der, die und das

The German for "the" is **der** before masculine nouns, **die** before feminine nouns and **das** before neuter nouns:

der Hund	the dog
die Blume	the flower
das Haus	the house

ein, eine

The German for "a" or "an" is **ein** before masculine and neuter words and **eine** before feminine nouns:

ein Hund	a dog
eine Blume	a flower
ein Haus	a house

Plurals

The word for "the" is **die** before all plural nouns (when you are talking about more than one person or thing):

die Hunde	the dogs
die Blumen	the flowers
die Häuser	the houses

Most German nouns change in the plural. Some add **n**, **e** or **er**, like the words above, but sometimes the vowel in the middle of the word changes too: **u** becomes **ü**, etc. You can see the plurals of nouns in the glossary like this:

der Hund(-e), **die Blume(-n)**, **das Haus(-er)**.

den, einen

All sentences have a subject and a verb. The subject is the person or thing doing the action (the verb). In some sentences the verb has an object too. This is the person or thing the action affects. When the object of a verb is a **der** word, the words for "the" and "a" change: **der** becomes **den** and **ein** becomes **einen**:

Ich esse den Kuchen. I am eating the cake.
Ich habe einen Hund. I have a dog.

Ich is the subject of the verb in both these sentences; **den Kuchen** and **einen Hund** are the objects.

Mein, **dein**, **sein** and **kein** always add the same endings as **ein**.

in, auf, unter . . .

Words like this, which tell you where things are, are called prepositions and usually come before a noun. The words for "the" and "a" change after them:

der and **das** both become **dem**
die (singular) becomes **der**
die (plural) becomes **den**
ein becomes **einem**
eine becomes **einer**

e.g. **auf dem Tisch** on the table
in der Ecke in the corner

In dem is often shortened to **im**, **zu dem** to **zum** and **zu der** to **zur**.

Pronouns

These are words which you use to replace nouns. There are three words for "you" in German: **du** (friendly), **ihr** (plural) and **Sie** (polite). There are also three words for "it". You use **er** for **der** words, **sie** for **die** words and **es** for **das** words.

				he/it			we
ich	I	**er**		he/it	**wir**		we
du	you (friendly)	**sie**		she/it	**ihr**		you (plural)
Sie	you (polite)	**es**		it	**sie**		they

Verbs

Verbs are "doing" words. German verbs change according to who is doing the action. Most of them follow a regular pattern and have the same endings. To learn a verb it helps to know the infinitive. This is its name, like "to eat" in English. German infinitives end in **en**, e.g. **gehen** (to go). With regular verbs you take the **en** off the infinitive, then add the different endings. You can see what they are in **gehen**, on the right.

gehen	to go
ich gehe	I go
du gehst	you go
er/sie/es/ geht	he/she/it goes
wir gehen	we go
ihr geht	you go (pl)
Sie gehen	you go (polite)
sie gehen	they go

Some verbs don't follow the usual pattern and it is best to learn them. You have already come across **sein** (to be) and **haben** (to have). Here are two of the other verbs you need to know.

sprechen	to speak
ich spreche	I speak
du sprichst	you speak
er/sie/es spricht	he/she/it speaks
wir sprechen	we speak
ihr sprecht	you speak (pl)
Sie sprechen	you speak (polite)
sie sprechen	they speak

essen	to eat
ich esse	I eat
du isst	you eat
er/sie/es isst	he/she/it eats
wir essen	we eat
ihr esst	you eat (pl)
Sie essen	you eat (polite)
sie essen	they eat

Separable verbs

Some German verbs are made up of two words. The infinitive is one word, but the verb often splits into the two words when it is used in a sentence.

Aufstehen (to get up) is made up of **auf** (up) and **stehen** (to stand). You use **stehen** like an ordinary verb, but **auf** usually goes to the end of the sentence:

Peter steht um acht Uhr auf. Peter gets up at eight o'clock.

Word order

In German sentences the verb always goes in second place. The subject of the sentence usually goes first:

Er geht zu Bett. He goes to bed.

but if something else, such as the time, comes first, the verb stays where it is and the subject of the sentence goes after it:

Um neun Uhr geht er zu Bett. He goes to bed at nine o'clock.

43

Answers to puzzles

p.7

What are they called?

Er heißt Peter. Sie heißt Sonja.
Sie heißen Klaus und Daniel.
Ich heiße (your name).

Who is who?

Helmut is talking to Fritz.
Anita is talking to Ingrid.
Helmut is next to the seal.
Fritz is talking to Helmut.
The girl in the bottom left-hand corner.
Michael is going home.

Can you remember?

Wie heißt du?
Ich heiße . . .
Das ist meine Freundin. Sie heißt Anita.
Mein Freund heißt Daniel.

p.9

Can you remember?

die/eine Blume, die/eine Katze,
der/ein Baum, das/ein Nest,
der/ein Vogel, das/ein Haus,
die Sonne, das/ein Fenster,
das/ein Auto, der/ein Hund.

p.11

Who comes from where?

Franz comes from Austria.
They are called Hari and Indira.
Yes, they are called Marie and Pierre.
No, she comes from Spain.
They come from India.
Yes, Angus comes from Scotland.
Pierre comes from France.
Yuri lives in Budapest.

Can you remember?

Woher kommst du?
Ich komme aus . . .
Ich spreche Deutsch.
Sprichst du Deutsch?

p.13

How old are they?

Michael is 13.
Petra and Sabine are 15.
Boris is 12.
Kirsten is 11.
Hugo is 9.
Barbara is 5.

How many brothers and sisters?

A = Petra and Sabine. B = Hugo. C = Michael.
D = Boris. E = Kirsten.

p.17

Where is everyone?

Stefan ist in der Küche.
Opa ist im Esszimmer.
Mutti ist im Schlafzimmer.
Peter ist im Badezimmer.
Heidi ist oben.
Das Gespenst ist im Heidis Zimmer.
Oma ist im Wohnzimmer.

Opa. Stefan. Peter. Mutti.

Im Wohnzimmer. In Heidis Zimmer.
Im Esszimmer. Im Badezimmer.

Ich bin hier oben. Ich bin in der Küche.

p.19

Where are they hiding?

Der Hamster ist in der Vase.
Das Kätzchen ist hinter dem Fernseher.
Das Hündchen ist im Schrank.
Der Wellensittich ist auf dem Bücherregal.
Die Schlange ist hinter dem Sofa.
Die Schildkröte ist neben dem Telefon.

p.21

Who likes what?

Boris. Johann. Bananen. Opa. Obsttorte.

p.23

Who is saying what?

"Ich habe Hunger."
"Guten Appetit!" "Bedien dich."
"Kannst du mir ein Glas reichen, bitte?"
"Möchtest du noch Pommes frites?"
"Ja, bitte. Ich mag Pommes frites."
"Nein, danke. Das reicht."
"Es schmeckt sehr gut."

p.25

What are they doing?

A Er kocht. B Er schwimmt. C Sie tanzen.
D Sie spielt Geige. E Er malt.

p.27

Hugo's day.

1b, 2e, 3f, 4a, 5h, 6g, 7d, 8c.

What time is it?

A Es ist fünf nach drei. B Es ist fünf nach elf.
C Es ist zehn vor neun. D Es ist Viertel vor vier.
E Es ist fünfundzwanzig nach drei. F Es ist halb
acht.
G Es ist drei Uhr. H Es ist vier Uhr.
I Es ist neun Uhr. J Es ist halb zwei.
K Es ist fünf nach sieben. L Es ist halb elf.
M Es ist sechs Uhr. N Es ist fünfundzwanzig vor
vier.
O Es ist fünf vor zwei.

p.29

On Friday evening I am going to the disco with
Boris.
I am playing tennis on Monday, Wednesday
and Sunday.
I am going to the cinema on Wednesday
evening.
Yes, I have a piano lesson on Tuesday.
Yes, I am free on Sunday morning.
It is at seven o'clock.

Schade, das geht nicht. Am Samstag
nachmittag spiele ich Fußball.

Ja, prima. Bis Donnerstag.

p.33

Entschuldigung. Wie komme ich zum
Marktplatz?
Entschuldigung. Gibt es hier in der Nähe
ein Café?
Ist es weit?

Nehmen Sie die dritte Straße links dann
fahren Sie geradeaus.

Nehmen Sie die dritte Straße rechts dann
gehen Sie geradeaus. Der Markt ist auf der
linken Seite.

To the shops.

p.37

Ich möchte vier Zitronen, ein Kilo Bananen
und eine Ananas, bitte.

Vier Zitronen kosten ein Euro sechzig.
Ein Kilo Bananen kostet ein Euro siebzig.
Eine Ananas kostet zwei Euro.

die Ananas. die Pfirsiche. die Zitronen. die
Orangen.

p.39

Hans hat am einundzwanzigsten Juli
Geburtstag.
Astrid hat am achtzehnten Oktober
Geburtstag.
Monika hat am einunddreißigsten August
Geburtstag.
Karl hat am dritten März Geburtstag.
Klaus hat am siebten September Geburtstag.

p.40

Die Straße ist grau. Die Sonne ist gelb.
Das Dach ist orange. Der Himmel ist blau.
Die Blumen sind rosa. Der Hund ist braun.
Der Vogel ist schwarz. Das Auto ist rot.
Die Bäume sind grün. Das Haus ist weiß.

Glossary

To find out what the plural of a word is, look at the letters in brackets after it. (-) means that the word doesn't change. (-e) or (-er) mean that you add "e" or "er" to the word. (ˉ) means that you add an umlaut to the main vowel in the word, or the last part of a long word: **der Vater** (ˉ) becomes **die Väter**, **das Schwimmbad (ˉer)** becomes **die Schwimmbäder**.

der Abend (-e)	evening
das Abendessen (-)	supper, tea
abends	in the evenings
aber	but
Afrika	Africa
alle	all
alt	old
am liebsten	best
am Meer	by the sea
an	on, by, in
die Ananas (-)	pineapple
der Apfel (ˉ)	apple
die Apotheke (-n)	chemist's
auch	also, too
auf	on top of, in
auf dem Land	in the country
auf deutsch	in German
auf englisch	in English
aufstehen	to get up
Auf Wiedersehen!	Goodbye!
aus	from, out of
außerdem noch etwas?	anything else?
das Auto (-s)	car
die Bäckerei (-en)	baker's
das Badezimmer (-)	bathroom
der Bahnhof (ˉe)	station
bald	soon
die Banane (-n)	banana
die Bank (-en)	bank
basteln	to make things
der Baum (ˉe)	tree
bedien dich	help yourself
bis	until, till
bis zum/zur	as far as
bitte	please
blau	blue
blond	blonde
die Blume (-n)	flower
braun	brown
das Brot (-e)	bread
das Brötchen (-)	bread roll
der Bruder (ˉ)	brother
das Buch (ˉer)	book
das Bücherregal (-e)	bookshelf
die Butter	butter
das Café (-s)	café
der Campingplatz (ˉe)	campsite
die Cola (-)	coca cola
das Dach (ˉer)	roof
da drüben	over there
danke	thank you
dann	then

dein, deine	your (sing.)
Deutsch	German
Deutschland	Germany
dick	fat
Dienstag	Tuesday
direkt	direct(ly)
die Disko	discotheque
Donnerstag	Thursday
dritter/e/es	third
dunkelhaarig	dark-haired
die Ecke (-n)	corner
das Ei (-er)	egg
ein bisschen	a little
einkaufen gehen	to go shopping
das Eis (-)	ice-cream
die Eltern (pl)	parents
England	England
Englisch	English
entlang	along
Entschuldigung	excuse me
erste	first
essen	to eat
das Esszimmer (-)	dining room
etwa	about
etwas	something
fahren	to drive
die Familie (-n)	family
fast	almost
das Fenster (-)	window
der Fernseher (-)	television
fernsehen	to watch television
finden	to find
der Fisch (-e)	fish
das Fleisch	meat
Frankreich	France
Französisch	French
Frau	Mrs.
Fräulein	Miss
Freitag	Friday
der Freund (-e)	friend(m)
die Freundin (-nen)	friend(f)
freundlich	friendly
der Frühling	Spring
das Frühstück	breakfast
furchtbar	terrible
Fußball spielen	to play football
ganz	quite, rather
die Garage (-n)	garage
gar nicht	not at all
der Geburtstag (-e)	birthday
gegenüber	opposite
gehen	to go
die Geige (-n)	violin

gelb	yellow	**kommen**	to come
die Gemüse (pl)	vegetables	**kosten**	to cost
geradeaus	straight ahead	**die Küche (-n)**	kitchen
gerne	with pleasure	**der Kuchen (-)**	cake
das Geschäft (-e)	shop		
die Geschwister (pl)	brothers and sisters	**das Lebensmittelgeschäft**	grocer's
das Gespenst (-er)	ghost	**lesen**	to read
gibt es . . . ?	is/are there?	**lieber**	better
das Glas (-̈er)	glass	**die Limonade (-n)**	lemonade
gleich	immediately	**links**	on the left
gleichfalls	the same to you	**das/der Liter (-)**	litre
grau	grey		
groß	tall	**machen**	to make, do
die Großeltern	grandparents	**malen**	to paint
die Großmutter (-̈)	grandmother	**der Markt (-̈e)**	market
der Großvater (-̈)	grandfather	**der Marktplatz (-̈e)**	market place
gut	good, well	**mein, meine**	my
Gute Nacht	Good Night	**die Metzgerei (-en)**	butcher's
Guten Abend	Good Evening	**die Milch**	milk
Guten Appetit!	Enjoy your meal!	**die Minute (-n)**	minute
Guten Tag	Good Day	**mit**	with
		der Mittag (-e)	noon, midday
haben	to have	**das Mittagessen (-)**	lunch
halb	half	**die Mitternacht**	midnight
der Hamburger (-)	hamburger	**Mittwoch**	Wednesday
der Hamster (-)	hamster	**mögen**	to like
das Haus (-̈er)	house	**der Monat (-e)**	month
der Herbst	Autumn	**Montag**	Monday
Herr	Mr.	**der Morgen (-)**	morning
heute	today	**morgen .**	tomorrow
hier	here	**morgens**	in the mornings
der Himmel	sky	**die Musik**	music
hinter	behind	**die Mutter (-̈)**	mother
das Hobby (-s)	hobby	**Mutti**	Mum
hören	to listen to		
der Hund (-e)	dog	**nach**	after, to
das Hündchen (-)	puppy	**der Nachmittag (-e)**	afternoon
Hunger haben	to be hungry	**nachmittags**	in the afternoons
		nächster/e/es	next
immer	always	**neben**	next to
in der Nähe	nearby	**nehmen**	to take
Indien	India	**nein**	no
das Instrument (-e)	instrument	**das Nest (-er)**	nest
		nicht	not
ja	yes	**noch**	more, still
das Jahr (-e)	year		
die Jugendherberge (-n)	youth hostel	**oben**	upstairs
jung	young	**das Obst**	fruit
		die Obsttorte (-n)	fruit tart
der Kaffee (-s)	coffee	**oder**	or
der Käse (-)	cheese	**Oma**	Granny
das Kätzchen (-)	kitten	**der Onkel (-)**	uncle
die Katze (-n)	cat	**Opa**	Grandad
kaufen	to buy	**orange**	orange
keine	not any, none	**die Orange (-n)**	orange
das Kilo (-s)	kilo	**der Orangensaft**	orange juice
das Kino (-s)	cinema	**Österreich**	Austria
die Kirche (-n)	church		
das Klavier (-e)	piano	**die Party (-s)**	party
klein	small	**der Pfennig (-e)**	penny
kochen	to cook	**der Pfirsich (-e)**	peach

die Pflanze (-n)	plant	suchen	to look for
das Pfund (-e)	half a kilo	der Supermarkt (¨)	supermarket
die Pizza (-s)	pizza		
die Pommes frites (pl)	chips	die Tankstelle (-n)	petrol station
die Post	post office	die Tante (-n)	aunt
die Postkarte (-n)	postcard	tanzen	to dance
prima!	that's great!	der Tee (-)	tea
		das Telefon (-e)	telephone
die Quiche	quiche	die Telefonzelle (-n)	phone box
		das Tennis	tennis
das Rathaus (¨er)	town hall	der Teppich (-e)	carpet
rechts	on the right	der Tisch (-e)	table
reichen	to pass	die Toiletten (pl)	toilets
der Reis	rice	die Tomate (-n)	tomato
rosa	pink	die Traube (-n)	grape
die Rose (-n)	rose	Tschüs!	Bye!
rot	red	die Tür (-en)	door
der Salat (-e)	salad	um	at
Samstag	Saturday	und	and
schade!	it's a shame!	Ungarn	Hungary
die Schildkröte (-n)	tortoise	unter	under
der Schinken	ham		
das Schlafzimmer (-)	bedroom	die Vase (-n)	vase
die Schlange (-n)	snake	der Vater (¨)	father
schlank	thin	Vati	Dad
das Schloss (¨er)	castle	das Verkehrsamt (¨er)	tourist office
die Schokolade	chocolate	der Vogel (¨)	bird
schön	beautiful	vor	in front of, to
der Schornstein (-e)	chimney	der Vorhang (¨e)	curtain
Schottland	Scotland		
der Schrank (¨e)	cupboard	wann?	when?
die Schule (-n)	school	was?	what?
schwarz	black	das Wasser	water
die Schwester (-n)	sister	weiß	white
das Schwimmbad (¨er)	swimming pool	weit	far
schwimmen	to swim	der Wellensittich (-e)	budgie
sehr	very	wer?	who?
sein	to be	wie?	how, what?
der Sessel (-)	armchair	der Winter	winter
das Sofa (-s)	sofa	wo?	where?
der Sommer	summer	woher?	where from?
die Sonne	sun	wohnen	to live
Sonntag	Sunday	die Wohnung (-en)	flat
sonst noch etwas?	anything else?	das Wohnzimmer (-)	living room
die Spaghetti	spaghetti	das Würstchen (-)	sausage
Spanien	Spain		
spielen	to play	zahlen	to pay
der Sport	sport	der Zaun (¨e)	fence
sprechen	to speak	ziemlich	quite, rather
die Stadt (¨e)	town, city	das Zimmer (-)	room
das Steak (-s)	steak	die Zitrone (-n)	lemon
die Straße (-n)	street	zu Fuß	on foot
stricken	to knit	zusammen	together
das Stück	piece, each	zwischen	between